WORKBOOK FOR

SECURE LOVE

(A Guide to Julie Menanno's Book)

We wish you the best of
luck and hope that this
book helps you achieve
your goals.

NOW IS THE TIME TO CHECK OUT THE TOP TIPS FOR BEING SUCCESSFUL IN USING THIS BOOK.

> ➤ Realize before you go any further that lying to <u>yourself is among the</u> worst things you can do. While following this guide, be honest with yourself.

> ➤ Use this guidance with caution and thoroughness while you seek out a guardian. It must be an accountable individual.

➤ **Engrave the book's teachings and principles deeply into your mind. It needs to permeate your entire being.**

➤ **When you get to the notes section, really let your thoughts flow.**

➤ **It is not an illusion; everything is actually feasible here.**

BEGINNING THE PROCESS OF CHANGE

A STATE OF MIND THAT COULD TRANSFORM

The beginning of a relationship is usually an exciting and pleasant time, but maintaining a relationship over time requires a lot of effort.

<u>Practical Steps You Can Do Right Now</u>

Once you're comfortable in your relationship, you need to keep the lines of conversation open and continue to enjoy your time with your partner.

DIFFICULTY WITH PERPETUAL

THOUGHT

Sometimes it's hard to
keep a relationship
going, but the benefits
of being in a committed
long-term relationship
far outweigh the problems
you may face.

Everything that is been occupying your thoughts

Though "date night" may seem forced, you and your partner should have one at least once a week, if not more. If "date night" seems too clichéd, then aim to spend at least one night a week alone together.

On date night, you may prepare supper and go to the movies, or try something new. While remaining in, light candles and play soothing music to create a romantic environment.

If you're going to spend time together, make sure you have time to really talk. If you're just going to a loud show together, you won't be able to talk much.

FINAL ARTICLE!

Learn how to say "no" when you're on a "date night." Even if your friends ask you to go out, if you have a date night planned, tell them you can't make it and plan something for next week.

A STATE OF MIND THAT COULD TRANSFORM

It is inevitable that things will fall apart if "date night" is the item that you are constantly prepared to give up.

Practical Steps You Can Do Right Now

It is important that you always look great, that you tell each other how much you love each other, and that you complement one other throughout the night.

DIFFICULTY WITH PERPETUAL

THOUGHT

Making love at least once
a week is important, no
matter how tired you are
after work or how busy
you are that week. You
don't have to write it
down on your calendar,
and hopefully you won't
have to.

Everything that is been occupying your thoughts

The act of making love is a means of preserving your connection with your spouse and of becoming closer to them.

It is also important that you spend some time just kissing and cuddling with each other so that you do not feel as like you are simply crossing "sex" off of your list of things to accomplish.

Sometimes your plans will get crazy, but you need to talk to each other every day, no matter how much work you have. You can plan to talk at dinner or over the phone if your friend or family member is not there.

FINAL ARTICLE!

Always know what your loved one did during the day. You don't have to tell each other about every little thing in your lives, but you should get used to each other's habits.

IT IS THE THIRD DAY OF YOUR TRANSFORMATION

A STATE OF MIND THAT COULD TRANSFORM

Spend at least fifteen minutes a day with your loved one and tell him how much you love and miss him if you're going to be apart for a week.

<u>Practical Steps You Can Do Right Now</u>

There shouldn't be anything else going on when you talk. You're not really talking if you check your phone or watch the game at the same time.

DIFFICULTY WITH PERPETUAL

THOUGHT

Being honest is important in any relationship that you want to last.[5] If you want your relationship to stay healthy, you should be able to tell your partner the truth.

<u>EVERYTHING THAT IS BEEN</u>
<u>OCCUPYING YOUR THOUGHTS</u>

When you're with someone you care about, you should be able to tell them your deepest thoughts and feelings.

Know what not to say. You should be honest with

your loved one most of
the time, but you don't
have to tell them
everything.

Time how honest you are.
Make sure you tell your
loved one about something

important when they have
time to talk and aren't
too stressed out.

FINAL ARTICLE!

He will be more open to
hearing your news if he
has time to do so.

FOURTH DAY OF YOUR
TRANSFORMATION

A STATE OF MIND THAT COULD TRANSFORM

When two people are close, being happy should matter more than being right.

Practical Steps You Can Do Right Now

If you want your relationship to last, you

should learn how to make
choices with your partner
and make sure that both
of you are happy with
them. You could also take
turns giving in to each
other.

DIFFICULTY WITH PERPETUAL

THOUGHT

Before you make a choice,
ask your loved one to
rate how important it is
to him on a scale from 1
to 10. Then, you should
say how important it is
to you.

Everything that is been occupying your thoughts

Next, you should discuss
the reasons why it is so

significant to both of
you, as well as the steps
you may take to make it
less significant.

Take some time to
reflect. Take the time to
examine the benefits and
drawbacks of the choice
that the two of you are
making together, as well

as what you can do to
find a middle ground.

Taking turns giving in to
minor choices is a good
idea. Instead of choosing
the movie for your date
night, you should allow

your girlfriend choose the restaurant.

FINAL ARTICLE!

Make sure that all parties are willing to compromise. You are not making a compromise if your lady is constantly giving in to what you want in the end because you are more persistent than she is.

This is Day 5 of Your Transformation

A STATE OF MIND THAT COULD TRANSFORM

It is extremely necessary to acquire the skill of expressing regret on a regular basis if you want to be in a relationship that will survive for a significant amount of time.

Practical Steps You Can Do Right Now

When it comes to a relationship, it is far more vital to say that you are sorry than it is to remain obstinate.

DIFFICULTY WITH PERPETUAL

THOUGHT

If you have done anything wrong,

you should learn how to apologize.

Everything that is been
occupying your thoughts

You may need some time to
come to the realization
that you have made a
mistake; nonetheless,
after you have done so,
you should express your
regret for what you have
done.

Be sure that you are
serious about it.
Maintain sincerity and
maintain eye contact.

Acquire the ability to accept the apologies of a loved one. If you honestly believe that he is sincere, then you should stop being so stubborn and instead accept his apologies and move on with your life.

FINAL ARTICLE!

At no point in time should you forget to tell someone "I love you" or take your sentiments for granted.

DAY 6 OF EMBRACING CHANGE

A STATE OF MIND THAT COULD TRANSFORM

Do not forget to express your affection for the person you care about on a daily basis; if you are able to do so, do it numerous times a day.

Practical Steps You Can Do Right Now

It is important to keep in mind that there is a distinction between the words "love you" and "I love you," and that you should really mean it when you say it.

DIFFICULTY WITH PERPETUAL

THOUGHT

Give your loved one
compliments at all times.
Please let her know how
much you like her smile
and how much you think
she looks amazing in her
new clothing.

Everything that is been
occupying your thoughts

Never fail to express to
your loved one how one-
of-a-kind they are.
Remember to always make
him feel like he is the
only one.

One may compare a relationship to a shark: if it does not progress, it will eventually perish. It is important that you discover strategies to maintain the vitality of your relationship so that your love does not become a mundane element of your time together.

Finding new hobbies that you and your partner can explore together is one approach to accomplish this goal.

FINAL ARTICLE!

This will provide you with something to be thrilled about as well as a passion that you both share.

DAY SEVEN OF YOUR JOURNEY TO TRANSFORMATION

A STATE OF MIND THAT COULD TRANSFORM

Attend a dancing lesson together on a weekly basis. In addition to providing you with a wonderful workout, this will also strengthen the passion that you have for one another.

Practical Steps You Can Do Right Now

Take any action that is outside of your comfort zone. Have a go at ice skating, mountain biking, or even trekking the trails.

DIFFICULTY WITH PERPETUAL

THOUGHT

Participating in an activity that is utterly foreign to you will bring you closer together.

Everything that is been occupying your thoughts

You need a healthy sex life to have a good relationship. After five years together, your lovemaking may not be as exciting as it was, but you should still attempt new things in the bedroom to keep it exciting.

Try making love in different ways. Even if what you've been doing works, don't keep doing it. You can even find new positions together, which is a great way to warm up.

Go to new places to make love. You don't have to sleep in the bedroom every time. Try the couch, the kitchen table, or even a hotel room during the day.

FINAL ARTICLE!

You could get some sexy things to bring into bed by going to a sex shop.

<u>WELL DONE!</u>

IT GIVES US GREAT PLEASURE
TO KNOW THAT YOU HAVE
REACHED THE CONCLUSION OF
THIS MANUAL.

EMBRACE WHAT YOU HAVE
LEARNED AND DO NOT LET IT
SLIP YOUR MIND.

DONATING COPIES IS A GREAT
WAY TO SHOW THAT YOU CARE
BY ALLOWING OTHERS TO
IMPROVE THEIR LIFE AS WELL.

Made in the USA
Las Vegas, NV
24 October 2024

10396550R00026